ZANZIBAR TRAVEL
2024 UPDATED

Explore Pristine Beaches, Historic Stone Town, and Authentic Swahili Culture - Discover the Hidden Charms, Exotic Cuisine, and Rich Cultural Tapestry of Zanzibar

Alexander Scott

0

Copyright ©2024 Alexander Scott

All rights reserved.

No part of this publication may be reproduced, distributed, or transmitted in any form or by any means, including photocopying, recording, or other electronic or mechanical methods, without the prior written permission of the publisher, except in the case of brief quotations embodied in critical reviews and certain other noncommercial uses permitted by copyright law.

ZANZIBAR TRAVEL GUIDE 2024 UPDATED

WELCOME TO ZANZIBAR

HISTORY OF ZANZIBAR

WHY ZANZIBAR SHOULD BE ON YOUR BUCKET LIST

WHAT YOU NEED FOR A TRIP TO ZANZIBAR

- THE TIME OF THE YEAR THAT IS MOST PREFERABLE FOR A VISIT
- WHAT ITEMS SHOULD BE CARRIED ALONG?
- VISA AND ENTRY REQUIREMENT
- ARRIVING THERE AND NAVIGATING YOUR SURROUNDINGS
- LANGUAGE BASIC YOU SHOULD KNOW BEFORE TRAVELLING TO ZANZIBAR

EXPLORING STONE TOWN

- HISTORIC SITES AND LANDMARKS
- MUSEUMS AND GALLERIES

SHOPPING AND MARKETS
DINING AND NIGHTLIFE

PLACES OF INTEREST FOR TOURISTS IN ZANZIBAR

10 EXCITING OUTDOOR ADVENTURES TO EXPERIENCES

10 AMAZING ITINERARIES FOR EVERY TOURIST

BEACH BUM BONANZA:
HISTORY BUFF'S DREAM:
SPICE ODYSSEY:
AQUATIC WONDERLAND:
SUNSET SAIL SERENADE:
PRIMATE PARADISE:
CULTURAL IMMERSION CRASH COURSE:
ISLAND HOPPING EXTRAVAGANZA:
KITE SURFING CARNIVAL:
SAFARI SPECTACULAR:

TOP ACCOMMODATION OPTION IN ZANZIBAR

10 BEST HOSTELS IN ZANZIBAR

FINEST RESTAURANT AND CUISINE EXPERIENCES IN ZANZIBAR

TOP SAVORY DISHES IN ZANZIBAR

10 BEST RESTAURANT IN ZANZIBAR

VIBRANT NIGHTLIFE AND FESTIVITY IN ZANZIBAR

FESTIVE CELEBRATIONS IN ZANZIBAR

EXPLORING ZANZIBAR SHOPPING AND SOUVENIR

TOP SHOPPING PLACES IN ZANZIBAR

CONCLUSION

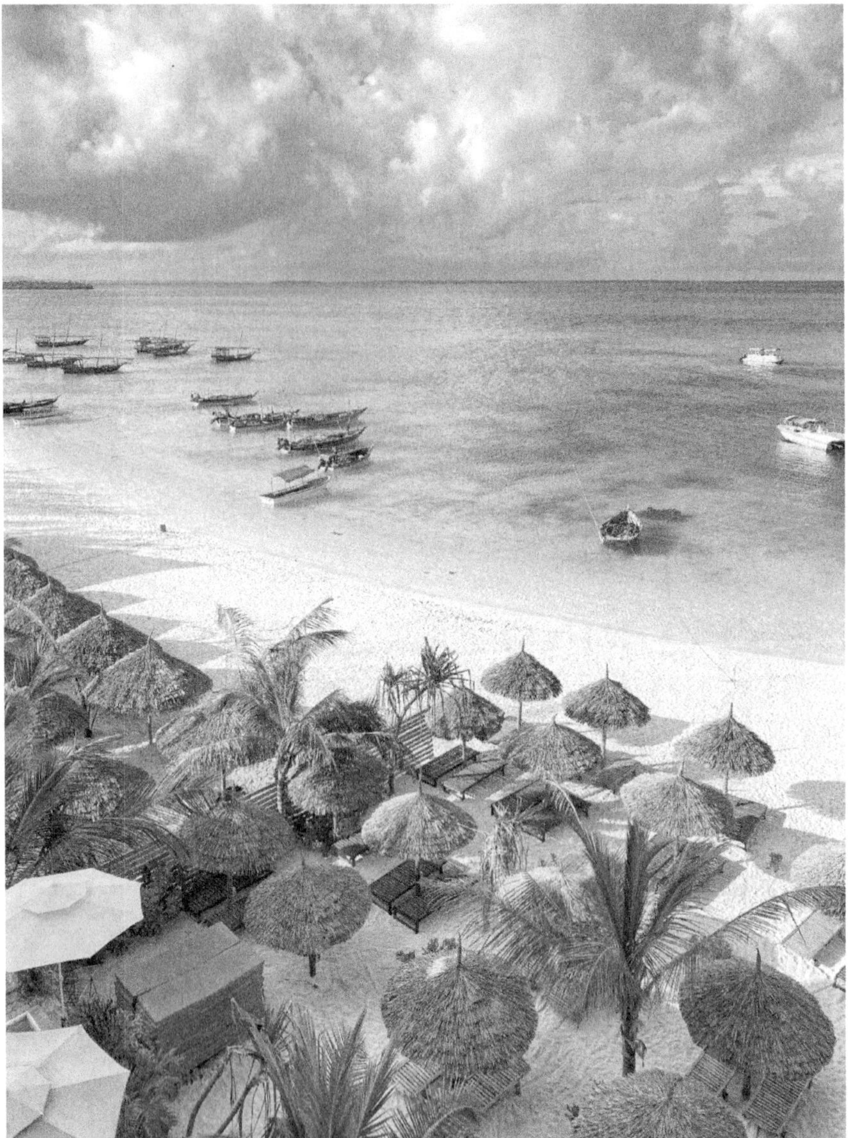

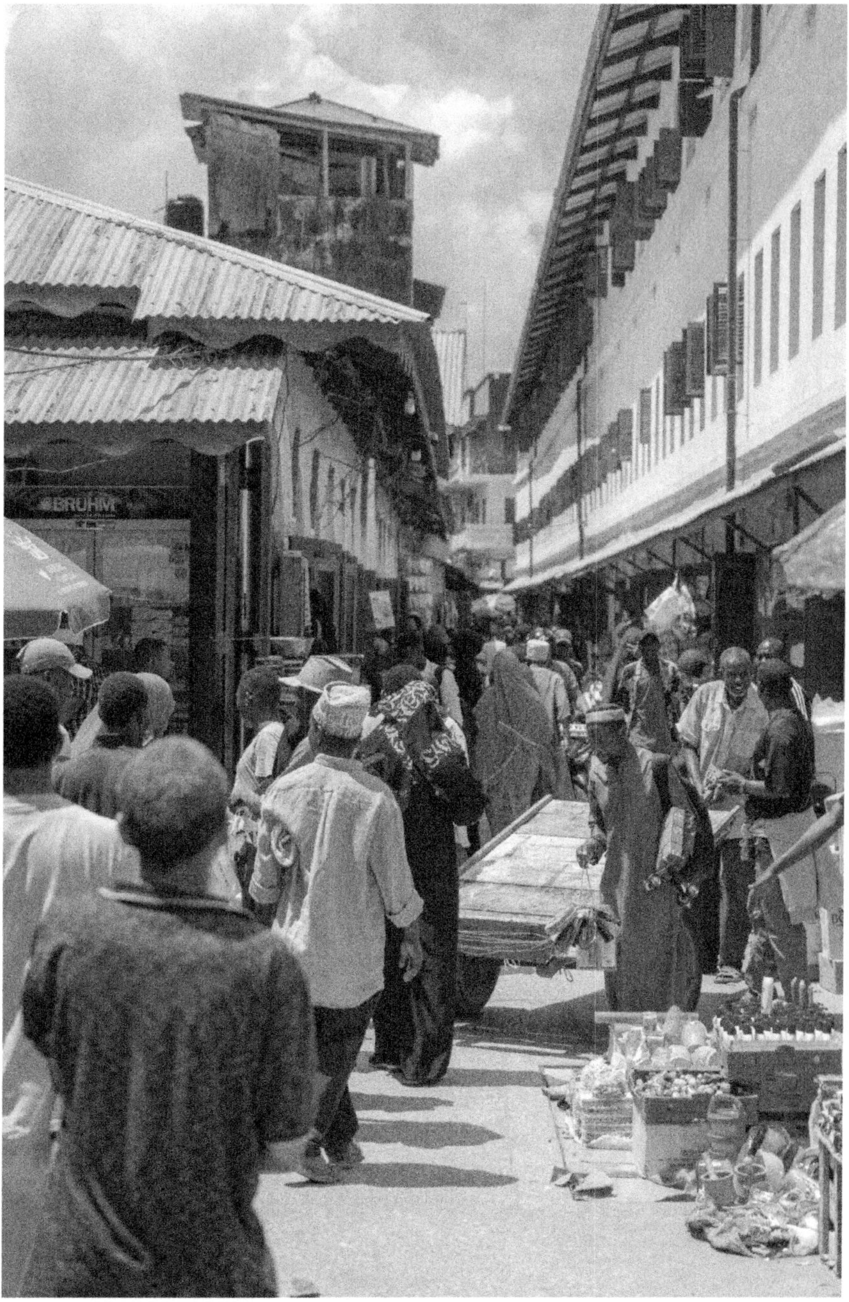
BRUHM

WELCOME TO ZANZIBAR

Welcome to Zanzibar, the exotic jewel of the Indian Ocean where history, culture, and natural beauty collide to create an unforgettable tropical paradise! As you step onto the shores of this enchanting island, prepare to be swept away by its vibrant colors, rich aromas, and warm hospitality. Whether you're a sun-seeking beach bum, a history buff, or an adventure enthusiast, Zanzibar has something special in store for you.

First things first, let's dive into the heart of Stone Town, the atmospheric and historic old quarter of Zanzibar City. Lose yourself in a maze of narrow streets lined with ancient buildings, bustling markets, and aromatic spice shops. Marvel at the intricate architecture of landmarks like the House of Wonders and the Old Fort, and immerse yourself in the island's multicultural heritage at the Palace Museum and the Arab Fort.

As you wander through the labyrinthine streets of Stone Town, be sure to visit the iconic Forodhani Gardens, where you can sample an array of delicious street food delights at the nightly food market. From grilled seafood skewers to mouthwatering Zanzibar pizzas, there's no shortage of culinary delights to tantalize your taste buds.

But Zanzibar isn't just about urban exploration – it's also home to some of the most stunning beaches and marine life in the world. Head north to Nungwi and Kendwa Beaches, where powdery white sands and crystal-clear turquoise waters await. Spend your days snorkeling, diving, or simply soaking up the sun on the pristine shores.

For a taste of adventure, embark on a spice tour and discover the island's rich agricultural heritage. Wander through lush spice plantations and learn about the cultivation of cloves, nutmeg, cinnamon, and vanilla. Take a guided tour of a local farm and sample exotic fruits straight from the tree, or indulge in a traditional Swahili cooking class and learn how to prepare authentic Zanzibari dishes using fresh spices and ingredients.

No visit to Zanzibar would be complete without exploring its fascinating underwater world. Strap on your snorkel or scuba gear and dive into the warm waters of the Indian Ocean, where you'll encounter vibrant coral reefs teeming with colorful fish, turtles, and other marine creatures. Head to Mnemba Atoll or Chumbe Island Marine Park for some of the best diving and snorkeling spots on the island.

And let's not forget about Zanzibar's rich cultural heritage – from the haunting beauty of the Slave Chambers to the tranquil serenity of the Jozani Chwaka Bay National Park. Explore the historic ruins of the Persian Baths and the Maruhubi Palace, or embark on a safari adventure to spot the island's unique wildlife, including red colobus monkeys, giant tortoises, and exotic bird species.

So whether you're seeking relaxation, adventure, or cultural immersion, Zanzibar has it all and more. So pack your bags, leave your worries behind, and get ready to embark on the adventure of a lifetime in this tropical paradise! Karibu Zanzibar – welcome to paradise!

WHY ZANZIBAR SHOULD BE ON YOUR BUCKET LIST

Imagine a place so steeped in enchantment that each step on its powdery sands feels like a dance with history, where the air is as rich with the scent of spices as it is with tales of ancient dhow sailors. This is Zanzibar, an island not just visited but deeply felt, a place where the sun doesn't set but rather sinks into the ocean in a display of colors so vibrant, you'll wonder if the sky is painting its masterpiece just for you.

Why visit Zanzibar? Because it's where adventure and relaxation meet in a perfect embrace. Here, the beaches are not just landscapes but canvases of nature's utmost artistry. The sand is so fine and white, it could be mistaken for a dusting of sugar by the uninitiated, and the sea a concoction of blues and greens so vivid, they make the rainbow look understated. You could spend days lounging on the beach, letting the waves whisper their secrets, or you could dive into those very waves, exploring coral reefs bustling with life, making friends with fish that carry the colors and patterns of a psychedelic dream.

And then there's Stone Town, the cultural heart of Zanzibar, a place where history doesn't just live, it thrives. Wandering through its narrow streets is like walking through a living museum, where every building, every door, and every cobblestone has a story to tell. It's a place where you can trace the footsteps of sultans, slaves, and sailors, all of whom have contributed to the rich tapestry that is Zanzibar's history. And as the sun dips below the horizon, casting shadows that dance along the coral walls, you'll find yourself lost in the sheer romance of it all.

But oh, the spices! Zanzibar is nicknamed the Spice Island for a reason. A visit here is a sensory overload, in the best way possible. The air is fragrant with cloves, cinnamon, nutmeg, and vanilla. A tour through a spice farm isn't just an education; it's an adventure for your senses, where you can see, touch, taste, and smell the very ingredients that have made Zanzibar famous across the globe. These spices have shaped the island's history, economy, and even its cuisine. Speaking of which...

The food in Zanzibar is a reflection of its melting pot culture, with influences from African, Arab, Indian, and European cuisines. It's where you can feast on fresh seafood straight from the Indian Ocean, seasoned with the island's own spices, and understand what it truly means to taste the flavor of a place.

But perhaps the most compelling reason to visit Zanzibar is its people. Warm, welcoming, and with smiles as bright as the Zanzibari sun, they are the soul of the island. Whether it's a fisherman sharing stories of the sea or a local guide revealing the secrets of Stone Town, the people you meet will add layers to your visit that no guidebook could ever capture.

In Zanzibar, every day is a story waiting to be written, a picture waiting to be painted, a memory waiting to be made. It's not just a place to visit. It's a world to be discovered, full of laughter, adventure, and the kind of beauty that doesn't just delight the eyes but feeds the soul.

So, why visit Zanzibar? Because in a world that often moves too fast, Zanzibar is a reminder of the magic that happens when you slow down and simply be. It's not just a destination; it's an experience, a feeling, a moment in time that stays with you long after you've left its shores. And that, dear traveler, is why Zanzibar beckons.

WHAT YOU NEED FOR A TRIP TO ZANZIBAR

THE TIME OF THE YEAR THAT IS MOST PREFERABLE FOR A VISIT

Ah, let me paint you a picture of the perfect time to visit Zanzibar! Close your eyes and imagine a world where the sun shines brightly, the skies are clear, and the air is filled with the sweet scent of spices. This, my friend, is Zanzibar at its finest.

The best time to visit this tropical paradise is during its two distinct seasons: the dry season and the rainy season. Let's break it down in a way that'll make you want to book your ticket ASAP.

Dry Season (June to October): Picture-perfect weather? Check. Warm temperatures? Double check. The dry season in Zanzibar is like stepping into a postcard brought to life. From June to October, the island basks in glorious sunshine, with clear skies and minimal rainfall. This is the ideal time for beach lovers and sun seekers to visit, as you'll have plenty of opportunities to soak up the sun, swim in the crystal-clear waters, and indulge in all the water sports your heart desires. Plus, with temperatures hovering around the mid-80s Fahrenheit (high 20s Celsius), you'll be living your best life without breaking a sweat.

But wait, there's more! June to October is also prime time for wildlife enthusiasts, as this is when humpback whales migrate through Zanzibar's waters, putting on a spectacular show for lucky onlookers. So grab your binoculars and get ready for some whale watching action!

Rainy Season (November to May): Now, don't let the name fool you; the rainy season in Zanzibar is anything but dreary. Sure, there may be some occasional showers, but they're usually short-lived and followed by glorious sunshine. Plus, the rainy season brings with it a whole host of perks that you won't find during the dry season.

From November to May, Zanzibar is a lush, green paradise bursting with life. The rains bring respite from the heat, turning the landscape into a verdant oasis teeming with blooming flowers and thriving wildlife. It's the perfect time to explore the island's lush interior, go on a spice tour, or take a leisurely stroll through the vibrant markets of Stone Town.

And let's not forget about the cultural festivals! The rainy season is festival season in Zanzibar, with events celebrating everything from music and dance to food and art. Immerse yourself in the local culture, sample traditional dishes, and dance the night away with the friendly locals.

WHAT ITEMS SHOULD BE CARRIED ALONG?

Adventurer, let's talk packing for your Zanzibar escapade! Imagine yourself as a modern-day explorer, embarking on a journey to uncover the treasures of this exotic island. What do you need to bring along for the ride? Let's dive in and find out!

First things first, let's talk attire. Picture yourself lounging on a pristine beach, the sun kissing your skin and the gentle breeze whispering through your hair. What are you wearing? Light, breathable fabrics are your best friends here. Think flowy sundresses, loose linen shirts, and comfortable shorts that allow you to move freely as you frolic in the sand or explore the winding streets of Stone Town.

Of course, no tropical adventure would be complete without swimwear! Pack your favorite swimsuits – the more colorful and vibrant, the better – and don't forget a stylish cover-up to throw on when you're ready to hit the beachside bars or explore beyond the shoreline.

Now, let's talk accessories. Sun protection is key, so don't forget your trusty sunglasses, wide-brimmed hat, and, of course, sunscreen with a high SPF. You'll also want to bring along a lightweight beach towel or sarong for lounging on the sand, as well as a reusable water bottle to stay hydrated under the African sun.

But wait, there's more! Zanzibar is a haven for water sports enthusiasts, so if you're planning on snorkeling, diving, or paddleboarding, don't forget to pack your gear. A snorkel mask and fins are essential for exploring the vibrant coral reefs and marine life that call Zanzibar's waters home.

And let's not forget about footwear! While flip-flops are perfect for sandy strolls along the beach, you'll want to bring along a pair of comfortable walking shoes for exploring Stone Town or venturing into the island's lush interior. And if you plan on hitting the dance floor at one of Zanzibar's lively beach parties, don't forget to pack your favorite dancing shoes!

VISA AND ENTRY REQUIREMENT

Now, let's start with the good news: Zanzibar welcomes travelers from far and wide with open arms, and many nationalities can enter visa-free or obtain a visa on arrival. Picture yourself as a passport-wielding hero, ready to conquer the seas and explore this exotic paradise.

First up, the lucky ones who can waltz into Zanzibar without a visa in hand! Citizens of countries such as the United States, the United Kingdom, Canada, Australia, and many European nations can rejoice, for they are granted a visa-free stay of up to 90 days upon arrival. It's as simple as flashing your passport and a winning smile at immigration, and voilà – you're in!

But what about those who need a little extra paperwork to secure their ticket to paradise? Fear not, for obtaining a visa for Zanzibar is a breeze! Many travelers can easily obtain a visa on arrival at the airport or port of entry, allowing them to dive headfirst into their Zanzibar adventure without a hitch.

Now, for the thrill-seekers who prefer to plan ahead, fear not – you can also apply for a visa in advance through the Tanzanian embassy or consulate in your home country. Simply gather your documents, fill out the necessary forms, and prepare yourself for the journey of a lifetime.

But wait, there's more! Zanzibar also offers an e-visa option for those who prefer to handle their travel documents with the click of a button. Simply hop online, fill out the application form, and await approval – it's that easy!

ARRIVING THERE AND NAVIGATING YOUR SURROUNDINGS

Ah, the journey to Zanzibar – an adventure in itself! Picture yourself as a modern-day explorer, charting a course to this exotic island paradise. But fear not, dear traveler, for getting to Zanzibar and moving around once you've arrived is as exhilarating as the destination itself!

Let's start with the journey to Zanzibar. Close your eyes and imagine yourself soaring through the skies, the wind in your hair and the promise of adventure on the horizon. Most travelers will arrive in Zanzibar by air, landing at Abeid Amani Karume International Airport in Unguja, the main island of Zanzibar. From here, it's just a short hop, skip, and jump to your hotel or beachside bungalow, where the real fun begins!

But what about those who prefer to take the scenic route? Fear not, for Zanzibar is also accessible by sea! Hop aboard a ferry from Dar es Salaam, Tanzania's bustling coastal city, and prepare yourself for a journey across the sparkling waters of the Indian Ocean. Keep your eyes peeled for dolphins dancing in the waves as you approach the shores of Zanzibar – it's a sight you won't soon forget!

Now, let's talk about moving around once you've arrived in Zanzibar. Whether you're exploring the historic streets of Stone Town or chasing waterfalls in the lush interior, getting around the island is a breeze – quite literally, if you opt for a breezy ride in a traditional dhow!

For those who prefer to keep their feet on solid ground, fear not – Zanzibar boasts a reliable network of taxis, daladalas (local minibuses), and boda bodas (motorcycle taxis) to whisk you away to your next adventure. Simply flag down a passing taxi, hop aboard a daladala bound for your destination, or hold on tight as your boda boda driver weaves through the bustling streets – the choice is yours!

But wait, there's more! No trip to Zanzibar would be complete without a leisurely stroll through the bustling markets of Stone Town. From the vibrant colors and intoxicating scents of the Darajani Market to the bustling activity of Forodhani Market by the sea, each step offers a glimpse into the vibrant culture and rich history of Zanzibar.

And let's not forget about the iconic bus stops and popular stops scattered throughout the island. Picture yourself hopping off the daladala at Mkokotoni Market, where vendors peddle fresh seafood and colorful produce, or disembarking at the Nungwi bus stop, just steps away from the pristine beaches and bustling beach bars of Zanzibar's northern coast.

LANGUAGE BASIC YOU SHOULD KNOW BEFORE TRAVELLING TO ZANZIBAR

Ahoy, language explorers! Get ready to dive into the colorful world of Swahili, the vibrant language spoken in Zanzibar and beyond. Whether you're bargaining at the markets, ordering food at a local eatery, or simply greeting the friendly locals, mastering a few key phrases will enhance your

17. **Ningependa kununua hii.** - *I would like to buy this. Navigate the markets like a pro by letting vendors know what catches your eye.*

18. **Nimepotea.** - *I'm lost. If you find yourself wandering off the beaten path, use this phrase to ask for directions.*

19. **Usiku mwema!** - *Good night! End your day on a positive note with this sweet farewell.*

20. **Hapa ni mzuri sana!** - *This place is very beautiful! Take in the breathtaking scenery of Zanzibar and share your appreciation with those around you.*

21. **Beba polepole, tafadhali.** - *Carry slowly, please. When transporting goods or luggage, use this polite request to ask for careful handling.*

22. **Twende!** - *Let's go! Get ready for adventure and rally your companions with this energetic call to action.*

23. **Nina njaa kama simba!** - *I'm hungry as a lion! Work up an appetite exploring Zanzibar's sights and sounds, then express your hunger with this playful comparison.*

24. **Baridi kama barafu!** - *Cold as ice! Cool off from the tropical heat by describing something chilly with this fun phrase.*

25. **Hakuna wifi!** - No wifi! Embrace the digital detox and disconnect from the online world with this humorous observation.

26. **Nzuri sana!** - Very beautiful! Marvel at the stunning landscapes and vibrant culture of Zanzibar, and express your admiration with this enthusiastic compliment.

27. **Niko hapa kwa furaha!** - I'm here with joy! Let the world know that you're embracing every moment of your Zanzibar adventure with this joyful declaration.

28. **Kunywa maji mengi!** - Drink plenty of water! Stay hydrated under the tropical sun by reminding yourself and others to drink plenty of water.

29. **Subiri kidogo.** - Wait a moment. Whether you're in line at a cafe or waiting for a friend, use this phrase to ask for a moment of patience.

30. **Ndiyo!** - Yes! Affirmative responses are easy with this simple and versatile word.

31. **Sio!** - No! When you need to decline an offer or express disagreement, use this straightforward word.

32. **Karibu nyumbani!** - *Welcome home! Make guests feel at ease and welcome in your home with this warm greeting.*

33. **Twiga!** - *Giraffe! Have fun learning animal names in Swahili, starting with the majestic giraffe.*

34. **Tumefika!** - *We have arrived! Arrive at your destination in style and announce your presence with this triumphant declaration.*

35. **Ngoja kidogo.** - *Wait a little. Patience is a virtue, and you can practice it with this gentle reminder to wait a bit longer.*

36. **Shauri yako!** - *It's up to you! Give someone the freedom to make their own choices with this empowering phrase.*

37. **Mzuri kama kawa!** - *Beautiful as always! Compliment someone on their appearance or work with this timeless praise.*

38. **Pole sana!** - *I'm very sorry! Express sincere apologies and empathy with this compassionate phrase*

39. . **Unapatikana wapi?** - *Where can you be found? If you're looking for someone or something specific, use this phrase to ask for their whereabouts.*

40. **Nina njaa kama mbwa mwitu!** - I'm hungry as a wolf! When hunger strikes, unleash your inner wolf and let everyone know it's time to eat.

41. **Nina usingizi.** - I am sleepy. If you're feeling tired after a day of exploring, use this phrase to express your need for some rest.

42. **Safari njema!** - Have a good trip! Bid farewell to travelers embarking on a journey with this well-wishing phrase.

43. **Kuna nini leo?** - What's happening today? Stay informed about events and activities by asking this question about the day's happenings.

44. **Fanya hivi.** - Do it like this. Offer guidance or instructions by demonstrating how something should be done.

45. **Karibu!** - Welcome! Extend a warm welcome to friends, family, and guests with this friendly greeting.

46. **Nina hamu ya kujifunza Kiswahili.** - I'm eager to learn Swahili. Show your enthusiasm for learning the local language with this statement.

47. **Ninaelewa.** - I understand. Let others know that you comprehend what's being said with this acknowledgment.

48. **Sitaki hii.** - I don't want this. Politely decline something you're offered by using this phrase.

49. **Niko hapa kwa muda mrefu.** - I'm here for a long time. Inform others about the duration of your stay with this statement.

50. **Kama unavyopenda.** - As you like it. Be flexible and accommodating by expressing willingness to go along with someone else's preferences.

EXPLORING STONE TOWN

Welcome to Stone Town, the historic heart of Zanzibar and a UNESCO World Heritage Site renowned for its winding alleyways, ancient architecture, and vibrant culture. Nestled along the shores of the Indian Ocean, this enchanting labyrinth of streets invites travelers to step back in time and explore a world where Swahili, Arab, Indian, and European influences converge in a tapestry of sights, sounds, and flavors. From its bustling markets and bustling waterfront to its ornate mosques and colonial-era buildings, Stone Town captivates visitors with its rich history, diverse cuisine, and warm hospitality. Whether you're wandering through the maze-like streets, savoring the spices of the local cuisine, or soaking up the sunset from a rooftop terrace, Stone Town promises an unforgettable journey through the heart and soul of Zanzibar. Welcome to a place where every corner tells a story and every moment is filled with wonder.

HISTORIC SITES AND LANDMARKS

1. **The Old Fort (Ngome Kongwe)**: Stand in awe of the imposing walls of The Old Fort, a majestic structure that has stood sentinel over Stone Town for over three centuries. Built by the Portuguese in the 17th century and later expanded by the Omani Arabs, this fortress

once protected the island from foreign invaders and served as a hub of trade and commerce. Today, it hosts cultural events, exhibitions, and the bustling Forodhani Night Market, where the scent of grilled seafood fills the air and the sounds of laughter echo through the ancient corridors.

2. **The House of Wonders (Beit al Ajaib)**: Marvel at the grandeur of The House of Wonders, a majestic palace that earned its name as the first building in Zanzibar to be electrified and the largest structure of its kind in East Africa. Built in the late 19th century as a symbol of modernity and progress, this iconic landmark now houses the Zanzibar National Museum of History and Culture, where visitors can explore exhibits on the island's rich heritage, from Swahili civilization to the era of Sultan Barghash.

3. **Freddie Mercury House**: Pay homage to one of Zanzibar's most famous sons at the Freddie Mercury House, the childhood home of the legendary Queen frontman. Tucked away on a quiet street in Stone Town, this humble abode is adorned with a plaque commemorating the rock icon's birthplace and serves as a pilgrimage site for fans from around the world. Channel your inner rockstar as you pose for photos outside the iconic blue

door and imagine the echoes of music that once filled the halls of this historic residence.

4. **The Anglican Cathedral of Christ Church**: Experience the solemn beauty of The Anglican Cathedral of Christ Church, a sacred sanctuary that stands as a poignant symbol of Zanzibar's abolitionist history. Built on the site of a former slave market, this Gothic-style cathedral commemorates the victims of the Arab slave trade and serves as a testament to the island's journey towards reconciliation and healing. Explore the tranquil interior, where shafts of sunlight filter through stained glass windows, illuminating the hushed whispers of prayer and reflection.

5. **The Sultan's Palace (Beit al-Sahel)**: Step into the opulent world of Zanzibar's sultans at The Sultan's Palace, a majestic residence that once served as the seat of power for the island's rulers. Built in the late 19th century by Sultan Barghash, this ornate palace features intricately carved doors, lush gardens, and a ceremonial throne room adorned with gold leaf and crystal chandeliers. Today, it houses the Palace Museum, where visitors can marvel at royal artifacts, ceremonial regalia, and the rich heritage of Zanzibar's monarchy.

6. **Forodhani Gardens**: Wander through the verdant oasis of Forodhani Gardens, a scenic waterfront park that serves as a beloved gathering place for locals and visitors alike. Originally a site for royal palaces and gardens, Forodhani is now a vibrant public space where families come to picnic, couples stroll hand in hand, and children play among the swaying palm trees and colorful flower beds. As the sun sets over the Indian Ocean, the gardens come alive with the sights and sounds of the nightly Forodhani Night Market, where vendors hawk fresh seafood, grilled meats, and sweet treats to hungry patrons.

7. **Beit el-Sahel (Palace Museum)**: Dive into the opulent world of Zanzibar's sultans at Beit el-Sahel, also known as the Palace Museum, a lavish residence-turned-museum that offers a glimpse into the island's royal past. Wander through ornately decorated rooms adorned with intricate woodcarvings, Persian rugs, and gilded furnishings, and imagine the grandeur of life within the walls of this historic palace. Discover artifacts, photographs, and royal regalia that tell the story of Zanzibar's monarchy, from its rise to power to its eventual decline.

8. **Emerson on Hurumzi**: Ascend to the rooftop of Emerson on Hurumzi and behold panoramic views of Stone Town's iconic

skyline, where minarets, domes, and coral-stone buildings stretch towards the heavens. Originally a merchant's mansion, this elegant hotel offers a glimpse into Zanzibar's storied past with its blend of Arabian, Indian, and Swahili architecture. Relax in the tranquil courtyard, adorned with lush foliage and bubbling fountains, or savor a traditional Swahili feast at the hotel's renowned rooftop restaurant, where the flavors of Zanzibar come alive against a backdrop of breathtaking vistas.

9. **Livingstone House**: Trace the footsteps of the legendary explorer at Livingstone House, a historic residence where Dr. David Livingstone once resided during his expeditions to East Africa in the 19th century. Perched on the edge of Stone Town's waterfront, this elegant mansion offers sweeping views of the Indian Ocean and serves as a reminder of Zanzibar's pivotal role in the age of exploration. Explore the museum exhibits and artifacts that chronicle Livingstone's adventures, from his encounters with African wildlife to his efforts to combat the Arab slave trade.

10. **The Mercury House (Beit al-Ajab)**: Pay tribute to one of Zanzibar's most famous sons at The Mercury House, the childhood home of legendary rock icon Freddie Mercury.

Nestled in the heart of Stone Town, this humble abode now serves as a museum and tribute to the Queen frontman, showcasing memorabilia, photographs, and personal belongings that celebrate his life and legacy. Step inside the colorful interiors and immerse yourself in the world of the iconic singer, whose music continues to inspire generations of fans around the globe.

MUSEUMS AND GALLERIES

1. **Palace Museum (Beit al-Sahel)**: Behold the grandeur of Zanzibar's royal past at the Palace Museum, housed within the Sultan's former residence, Beit al-Sahel. Wander through ornately decorated rooms adorned with Persian rugs, gilded furniture, and intricate carvings, as you learn about the island's storied history and the lives of its rulers. Marvel at the Sultan's ceremonial throne, explore the harem quarters, and stroll through the lush gardens, where echoes of bygone days linger in the tropical breeze.

2. **Zanzibar Gallery**: Dive into the vibrant world of contemporary African art at the Zanzibar Gallery, a showcase of local talent and creativity. Admire colorful paintings, sculptures, and mixed-media works that capture the spirit of Zanzibar's landscapes, culture, and people. From bold abstracts to intricate designs, each piece tells a story of

resilience, beauty, and diversity, inviting you to explore the rich artistic heritage of the island.

3. **House of Wonders (Beit-al-Ajaib)**: Uncover the mysteries of Zanzibar's past at the House of Wonders, a majestic palace that once served as the seat of the Sultanate's government. Marvel at its iconic clock tower and ornate facade, then step inside to explore its fascinating exhibits on Swahili culture, maritime history, and colonial legacy. From ancient artifacts to interactive displays, the House of Wonders offers a captivating glimpse into the island's cultural heritage and architectural marvels.

4. **Zanzibar Butterfly Centre**: Immerse yourself in the beauty of nature at the Zanzibar Butterfly Centre, a tropical oasis where colorful butterflies flutter amidst lush gardens and exotic flowers. Wander through the butterfly enclosure and marvel at the dazzling array of species from around the world, as knowledgeable guides share fascinating facts about their life cycles, behaviors, and habitats. With its serene ambiance and breathtaking beauty, the Zanzibar Butterfly Centre is a must-visit destination for nature lovers and photography enthusiasts alike.

5. **Maritime Museum**: Set sail on a voyage of discovery at the Maritime Museum, where the sea-faring history of Zanzibar comes to life through artifacts, models, and interactive exhibits. Learn about the island's rich maritime heritage, from its role as a trading hub along the ancient Spice Route to its connection to the slave trade and colonial expansion. Explore replicas of traditional dhows, navigational instruments, and historical documents that trace the evolution of Zanzibar's seafaring culture and maritime traditions.

6. **Dhow Countries Music Academy (DCMA)**: Let the rhythm of Zanzibar captivate your soul at the Dhow Countries Music Academy (DCMA), a cultural institution dedicated to preserving and promoting the island's musical heritage. Attend live performances and workshops showcasing traditional taarab, ngoma, and mchiriku music, as talented musicians and dancers bring centuries-old rhythms to life. From soulful melodies to lively beats, the DCMA offers a sensory feast for music lovers and cultural enthusiasts eager to experience the heartbeat of Zanzibar.

7. **Princess Salme Museum**: Delve into the fascinating life of Princess Salme, daughter of Sultan Said bin Sultan Al-Busaid, at the

Princess Salme Museum. Housed within the former residence of the Zanzibari princess, this museum offers a glimpse into her extraordinary journey from royal heiress to European exile. Explore her personal belongings, letters, and photographs, as well as exhibits on Zanzibar's history, culture, and the enduring legacy of Princess Salme's remarkable story.

8. **Mnazi Mmoja Park and Peace Memorial Museum**: Pay tribute to Zanzibar's struggle for independence and the victims of the 1964 revolution at Mnazi Mmoja Park and Peace Memorial Museum. Stroll through the tranquil park, home to towering baobab trees and lush greenery, before visiting the museum to learn about the island's turbulent past and the quest for peace and reconciliation. With its thought-provoking exhibits and serene surroundings, Mnazi Mmoja Park offers a space for reflection and remembrance in the heart of Stone Town.

SHOPPING AND MARKETS

First stop, the iconic Darajani Market, where the air is filled with the intoxicating aroma of spices and the chatter of vendors haggling over their wares. Lose yourself in a maze of stalls piled high with fresh fruits, vegetables, and seafood, as well as an array of spices that will tantalize your senses and transport you to distant lands.

Next, we'll wander through the narrow alleys of the Forodhani Night Market, where the scent of grilled seafood mingles with the sounds of sizzling skewers and lively conversation. Sample street food delights like Zanzibar pizza, grilled lobster, and sugarcane juice, all freshly prepared and bursting with flavor. Don't forget to try the local favorite, urojo, a tangy soup made with lentils, potatoes, and coconut milk – it's a true taste of Zanzibar!

As we meander through the labyrinthine streets of Stone Town, we'll stumble upon hidden gems like the Maka Market, where local artisans showcase their handicrafts and artwork. From intricately carved wooden sculptures to colorful textiles and beaded jewelry, you'll find unique treasures that make perfect souvenirs of your time in Zanzibar.

For a taste of the island's rich cultural heritage, we'll visit the bustling streets of the Mwanakwerekwe Market, where vendors sell traditional fabrics like khangas and kitenges adorned with vibrant patterns and Swahili proverbs. Pick out a few pieces to add a touch of Zanzibari flair to your wardrobe, or simply admire the skill and artistry of the local craftsmen.

No shopping excursion in Stone Town would be complete without a visit to the Zanzibar Curio Shop, a treasure trove of souvenirs and gifts that capture the spirit of the island. Browse through shelves filled with handcrafted goods, including beaded sandals, woven baskets, and carved wooden figurines depicting local wildlife and cultural motifs. Admire the intricate designs of traditional Maasai jewelry, and pick out a few pieces to adorn yourself or your loved ones back home.

DINING AND NIGHTLIFE
Restaurants:

1. **Forodhani Gardens Food Market**: Dive into the culinary delights of Zanzibar at the iconic Forodhani Gardens Food Market. As the sun sets, this waterfront promenade transforms into a bustling food market where vendors grill, fry, and skewer a mouthwatering array of seafood, meats, and snacks. Sample street food favorites like grilled lobster, seafood kebabs, and Zanzibar pizzas stuffed with spicy fillings, all while soaking up the lively atmosphere and stunning views of the Indian Ocean.

2. **Emerson Spice Tea House**: Step back in time at the Emerson Spice Tea House, a historic mansion turned restaurant that offers a taste of Zanzibar's colonial past. Indulge in a sumptuous Swahili feast served on antique silverware, surrounded by ornate furniture and traditional decor. From aromatic curries to fragrant rice dishes, each bite is a culinary journey through Zanzibar's rich cultural heritage.

3. **6 Degrees South**: Elevate your dining experience at 6 Degrees South, a stylish restaurant located at the Serena Hotel. With its panoramic views of the Indian Ocean and chic ambiance, this upscale eatery offers a modern twist on traditional Zanzibari cuisine. Savor dishes made with locally sourced ingredients, such as coconut-crusted prawns, grilled octopus, and spice-infused tagines, all expertly prepared by the hotel's talented chefs.

4. **Lukmaan Restaurant**: For a taste of authentic Zanzibari home cooking, head to Lukmaan Restaurant, a popular spot among locals and tourists alike. This no-frills eatery serves up hearty dishes like biryani, pilau, and chapati, as well as fresh seafood and vegetarian options. Don't miss the chance to try their famous Zanzibar mix, a mouthwatering platter of grilled seafood, samosas, and salads that's perfect for sharing.

Nightlife:

1. **Mercury's**: Channel your inner rockstar at Mercury's, a lively bar named in honor of Zanzibar's most famous son, Freddie Mercury. Located at the Emerson Spice Hotel, this atmospheric venue features live music performances, themed parties, and a rooftop terrace with stunning views of Stone Town. Sip on creative cocktails inspired by the

legendary Queen frontman as you dance the night away to classic rock hits and chart-topping tunes.

2. **Monsoon Restaurant & Bar**: Immerse yourself in the exotic ambiance of Monsoon Restaurant & Bar, a hidden gem tucked away in the heart of Stone Town. With its eclectic decor and laid-back vibe, this intimate venue offers a cozy retreat from the bustling streets outside. Enjoy signature cocktails crafted with fresh fruits and local spices, accompanied by live music and cultural performances that showcase the diverse rhythms of Zanzibar.

3. **Livingstone Beach Restaurant & Bar**: For beachside vibes and sunset views, head to Livingstone Beach Restaurant & Bar on the shores of Nungwi Beach. This popular hangout spot offers a relaxed atmosphere where you can kick back with a cold drink in hand and watch the waves roll in. Enjoy live music performances by local bands and DJs, or join in the nightly bonfires and drum circles that light up the beach.

4. **Taperia Wine & Tapas Bar**: Transport yourself to Spain at Taperia Wine & Tapas Bar, a charming venue that specializes in Spanish-inspired cuisine and fine wines. Located in the heart of Stone Town, this cozy bar offers an extensive selection of tapas,

pintxos, and cheese boards, paired with an impressive array of wines from around the world. Whether you're sipping sangria on the terrace or sampling sherry by the bar, Taperia promises a taste of European elegance in the heart of Zanzibar.

Direction

Forodhani Gardens Food Market
Address: Forodhani Gardens, Stone Town, Zanzibar.

Emerson Spice Tea House
Address: Emerson Spice Hotel, Tharia Street, Stone Town, Zanzibar

6 Degrees South
Address: Serena Hotel, Kelele Square, Stone Town, Zanzibar

Lukmaan Restaurant
Address: Kenyatta Road, Stone Town, Zanzibar

Mercury's
Address: Emerson Spice Hotel, Tharia Street, Stone Town, Zanzibar

Monsoon Restaurant & Bar
Address: Gizenga Street, Stone Town, Zanzibar

Livingstone Beach Restaurant & Bar
Address: Nungwi Beach, Zanzibar

Taperia Wine & Tapas Bar

Address: Taperia Wine & Tapas Bar, Shangani Street, Stone Town, Zanzibar

PLACES OF INTEREST FOR TOURISTS IN ZANZIBAR

Alright, fellow adventurer, buckle up and get ready for a whirlwind tour of unforgettable places to visit in Zanzibar! From historic landmarks to natural wonders and everything in between, this island paradise is bursting at the seams with excitement and adventure. So grab your sunscreen, slip on your shades, and let's dive in!

1. **Stone Town**: Step back in time as you wander the labyrinthine streets of Stone Town, a UNESCO World Heritage Site steeped in history and culture. Lose yourself in the maze of narrow alleys lined with intricately carved doors, bustling markets, and historic landmarks.

2. **Prison Island**: Escape to Prison Island, a tropical paradise just a short boat ride from Stone Town. Explore the island's pristine beaches, swim in crystal-clear waters, and visit the famous Aldabra giant tortoises that call the island home.

3. **Jozani Forest**: Immerse yourself in nature at Jozani Forest, Zanzibar's only national park. Trek through lush mangrove forests, spot endemic wildlife such as the rare red colobus monkeys, and marvel at the beauty of this ecological treasure.

4. **Nungwi Beach**: Sink your toes into the soft, powdery sands of Nungwi Beach, located on the northern tip of the island. With its turquoise waters, swaying palm trees, and vibrant beach bars, it's the perfect spot to soak up the sun and unwind in paradise.

5. **Kendwa Beach**: Dance the night away under the stars at Kendwa Beach, known for its lively beach parties and vibrant nightlife. Whether you're sipping cocktails by the sea or busting a move on the dance floor, Kendwa Beach is the place to see and be seen after dark.

6. **Mnemba Atoll**: Dive into a world of underwater wonders at Mnemba Atoll, a pristine marine reserve teeming with colorful coral reefs and exotic marine life. Whether you're snorkeling, diving, or simply soaking up the sun on a secluded sandbank, Mnemba Atoll is a paradise for water lovers.

7. **Spice Farms**: Embark on a sensory journey through Zanzibar's spice farms, where you can see, smell, and taste the island's famous spices up close. From cloves and cinnamon to nutmeg and vanilla, discover the secrets behind Zanzibar's spice trade and sample exotic flavors straight from the source.

8. **Chumbe Island Coral Park**: Experience eco-tourism at its finest at Chumbe Island Coral Park, a protected marine sanctuary and

forest reserve. Explore pristine coral reefs, hike through lush mangrove forests, and stay in sustainable eco-bungalows overlooking the turquoise waters of the Indian Ocean.

9. **Forodhani Gardens**: Indulge your taste buds at Forodhani Gardens, a bustling night market located on the seafront in Stone Town. Sample a mouthwatering array of street food delights, from fresh seafood skewers and Zanzibari pizza to sugarcane juice and sweet treats.

10. **Mangapwani Slave Chambers**: Pay tribute to Zanzibar's history at the Mangapwani Slave Chambers, a haunting reminder of the island's dark past. Explore underground chambers where enslaved Africans were held before being shipped off to distant lands, and learn about Zanzibar's role in the slave trade.

11. **Old Fort**: Step back in time at the Old Fort, a 17th-century fortress located in the heart of Stone Town. Climb to the top of the battlements for panoramic views of the city, explore the cultural center and handicraft markets within the fort walls, and catch a traditional Taarab music performance under the stars.

12. **Nakupenda Beach**: Escape the crowds and discover your own slice of paradise at

Nakupenda Beach, also known as "Love Island." With its pristine white sands, crystal-clear waters, and stunning views of the mainland, Nakupenda Beach is the perfect spot for a romantic getaway or a peaceful day of relaxation.

13. **Mafia Island**: Venture off the beaten path and explore the untouched beauty of Mafia Island, located just a short flight or ferry ride from Zanzibar. Dive with whale sharks, snorkel in coral gardens, and soak up the laid-back island vibes on this hidden gem in the Indian Ocean.

14. **Maruhubi Palace Ruins**: Uncover the secrets of Zanzibar's royal past at the Maruhubi Palace Ruins, once the lavish residence of Sultan Barghash. Explore the crumbling remains of the palace, wander through overgrown gardens, and imagine life in Zanzibar's golden age of sultans and spice traders.

15. **Paje Beach**: Feel the wind in your hair and the sand between your toes at Paje Beach, a paradise for kitesurfers and beach lovers alike. Whether you're soaring through the air on a kiteboard or simply lounging in a hammock under the shade of a palm tree, Paje Beach is the ultimate destination for sun, sea, and adventure.

10 EXCITING OUTDOOR ADVENTURES TO EXPERIENCES

Ahoy, fellow adventurer! Get ready to unleash your inner thrill-seeker with these 10 exciting outdoor adventures in Zanzibar. From heart-pounding activities to awe-inspiring natural wonders, this island paradise is a playground for the adventurous soul. So strap on your boots, grab your gear, and let's dive into the excitement!

1. **Snorkeling with Whale Sharks**: Ever dreamed of swimming alongside the gentle giants of the sea? Zanzibar offers the chance to snorkel with whale sharks, the largest fish in the ocean. Join a guided tour and embark on an unforgettable underwater adventure as you encounter these majestic creatures in their natural habitat.

2. **Kiteboarding in Paje**: Feel the wind in your hair and the rush of adrenaline as you take to the skies with kiteboarding in Paje. With its shallow, turquoise waters and consistent trade winds, Paje Beach is the perfect spot for beginners and experienced kiteboarders alike to soar through the air and ride the waves.

3. **Rock Climbing at Nungwi Caves**: Channel your inner daredevil and conquer the towering limestone cliffs of Nungwi Caves. With routes

for climbers of all skill levels, this natural rock climbing paradise offers breathtaking views of the ocean and the chance to push your limits in a stunning coastal setting.

4. **Dhow Sailing Excursion**: Set sail on a traditional dhow boat and embark on a scenic sailing excursion around the pristine waters of Zanzibar. Whether you're cruising along the coast, exploring hidden coves, or watching the sunset over the Indian Ocean, a dhow sailing adventure is an unforgettable way to experience the beauty of the island.

5. **Zip-lining in Jozani Forest**: Take your sense of adventure to new heights with zip-lining through the treetops of Jozani Forest. Strap in and soar through the canopy, zipping from platform to platform as you take in panoramic views of the lush jungle below and keep an eye out for rare wildlife such as red colobus monkeys.

6. **Quad Biking in the Countryside**: Get off the beaten path and explore the rugged terrain of Zanzibar's countryside on a quad biking adventure. Zoom along dirt tracks, traverse sandy trails, and discover hidden gems as you navigate through picturesque villages, lush farmland, and scenic landscapes.

7. **Deep Sea Fishing Expedition**: Cast your line and reel in the catch of a lifetime on a

deep-sea fishing expedition in the waters surrounding Zanzibar. Whether you're targeting marlin, sailfish, or tuna, the nutrient-rich waters of the Indian Ocean offer world-class fishing opportunities for anglers of all skill levels.

8. **Caving at Kiwengwa Caves**: Delve into the depths of Kiwengwa Caves and uncover the mysteries hidden beneath the surface. Navigate through labyrinthine tunnels, squeeze through narrow passages, and marvel at stalactites and stalagmites as you explore this fascinating underground world.

9. **Mountain Biking in Chwaka Bay**: Pump up your adrenaline and hit the trails on a mountain biking adventure in Chwaka Bay. Navigate through mangrove forests, pedal along coastal tracks, and soak up the stunning scenery as you ride through one of Zanzibar's most scenic and diverse landscapes.

10. **Sunset Safari in Michamvi**: Embark on a sunset safari and experience the beauty of Zanzibar's countryside in the golden hour. Hop aboard a safari vehicle and journey through rural villages, rolling hills, and lush farmland as you chase the setting sun and soak up the breathtaking views of the island.

10 AMAZING ITINERARIES FOR EVERY TOURIST

Ahoy, fellow traveler! Prepare to be dazzled by these 10 amazing itineraries crafted to cater to every preference under the sun. From beach bums to history buffs, adventure seekers to foodies, Zanzibar has something special in store for everyone. So grab you camera pack your sense of adventure, and let's dive into these unforgettable journeys through paradise!

Beach Bum Bonanza:

Let's kick off with some serious beach time at Nungwi Beach. Picture this: warm sand between your toes, the sun kissing your skin, and the rhythmic sound of waves lulling you into bliss. Don't forget to snap some envy-inducing selfies with the iconic Zanzibari dhows bobbing in the background.

History Buff's Dream:

Dive deep into the historical tapestry of Stone Town. Roam the labyrinthine streets lined with centuries-old buildings boasting intricate Arabesque architecture. Marvel at the imposing fortresses of Old Fort and Beit el-Ajaib, and lose yourself in the bustling alleys of Darajani Market.

Spice Odyssey:

Prepare your senses for a tantalizing adventure through Zanzibar's spice plantations. Wander through lush fields bursting with cinnamon, cloves, and vanilla. Engage in a sensory feast as you touch, smell, and taste exotic spices straight from the source. Pro tip: grab a bag of freshly ground spices to spice up your culinary creations back home!

Aquatic Wonderland:

Strap on your snorkeling gear and get ready for an underwater escapade in Mnemba Atoll. Dip into the crystal-clear waters teeming with vibrant marine life—think technicolor coral reefs, playful dolphins, and maybe even a sea turtle or two. It's like snorkeling in a real-life aquarium!

Sunset Sail Serenade:

Set sail aboard a traditional dhow boat and let the evening unfold in a magical symphony of colors. Glide over the gentle waves as the sun dips below the horizon, painting the sky in hues of orange and pink. Indulge in a sumptuous seafood dinner served on deck, accompanied by the soothing melodies of Swahili music.

Primate Paradise:

Channel your inner Jane Goodall and embark on a quest to spot the elusive Zanzibar red colobus monkey in Jozani Forest. Trek through dense foliage, keeping your eyes peeled for these charismatic creatures swinging from branch to branch. Bonus points for spotting other forest dwellers like the adorable Sykes' monkeys!

Cultural Immersion Crash Course:

Immerse yourself in the vibrant tapestry of Zanzibari culture with a visit to a local village. Engage in lively conversations with friendly locals, learn traditional dances, and try your hand at cooking authentic Swahili dishes. It's not just a cultural exchange—it's a heartfelt connection with the soul of Zanzibar.

Island Hopping Extravaganza:

Hop aboard a boat and set sail to explore the pristine islands dotting Zanzibar's coastline. Marvel at the giant tortoises roaming freely on Prison Island, snorkel amidst colorful coral gardens at Chumbe Island Coral Park, and soak up the laid-back vibes of Bawe Island. Each island is a slice of paradise waiting to be discovered!

Kite Surfing Carnival:

Calling all adrenaline junkies! Head to Paje Beach, Zanzibar's kite surfing mecca, and prepare for an adrenaline-fueled adventure on the waves. Feel the wind in your hair as you glide across the turquoise lagoon, executing jaw-dropping tricks and maneuvers like a pro. Who needs gravity when you can fly on water?

Safari Spectacular:

Extend your Zanzibar escapade with an epic safari adventure on the mainland. Embark on a thrilling safari drive through Tanzania's iconic national parks, from the vast plains of the Serengeti to the wildlife-rich Ngorongoro Crater. Get ready for close encounters with Africa's Big Five and a front-row seat to the greatest show on earth—the Great Migration!

TOP ACCOMMODATION OPTION IN ZANZIBAR

10 BEST HOSTELS IN ZANZIBAR

If you're on a budget but still craving a slice of paradise, fear not! Here's a detailed guide to the 10 best hostels in Zanzibar, where affordability meets awesome vibes:

1. **Chillax Hostel Zanzibar**: Nestled in the heart of Stone Town, this hostel is all about laid-back vibes and friendly faces. Picture colorful murals, hammocks swaying in the breeze, and rooftop views that will leave you breathless. With comfy dorms and a communal kitchen perfect for whipping up budget-friendly meals, Chillax is the ultimate backpacker's haven.

2. **Zanziplanet Hostel**: Located just steps away from the white sands of Nungwi Beach, Zanziplanet offers a beachfront paradise without breaking the bank. Spend your days soaking up the sun, lounging in the hostel's beachside garden, or mingling with fellow travelers over a game of beach volleyball. Don't forget to catch the epic sunset views from the rooftop terrace!

3. **Lost & Found Hostel**: Get lost in the charm of Jambiani village at Lost & Found Hostel,

where rustic chic meets laid-back luxury. Tucked away amidst swaying palm trees and turquoise waters, this eco-friendly hostel offers cozy bamboo bungalows and beachside bonfires under the stars. It's the perfect spot to unwind and reconnect with nature.

4. **Savanna & Ocean**: If you're seeking a taste of authentic Zanzibari culture, look no further than Savanna & Ocean Hostel in Paje. Set in a traditional Swahili house with a lush garden oasis, this hostel offers a cultural immersion like no other. Learn to cook Swahili delicacies, jam with local musicians, and sip fresh coconut water straight from the tree.

5. **Zanzibar Rock House**: For the adventurous souls seeking a taste of the high life, Zanzibar Rock House is your ticket to rooftop bliss. Perched atop a historic building in Stone Town, this hostel boasts panoramic views of the Indian Ocean and the city skyline. Spend your evenings stargazing from the rooftop terrace or swapping travel tales with fellow explorers.

6. **Jambiani Guesthouse**: Experience the best of both worlds at Jambiani Guesthouse, where budget-friendly dorms meet boutique hotel vibes. Located in the heart of Jambiani village, this charming hostel offers stylish accommodations, a refreshing swimming

pool, and a lively bar scene that keeps the good times rolling long into the night.

7. **Paje by Night**: Dive into the vibrant beach culture of Paje at Paje by Night Hostel, where every day feels like a tropical adventure. With direct beach access, a buzzing beach bar, and daily yoga sessions overlooking the ocean, this hostel is a haven for sun seekers and soul searchers alike. Plus, you can try your hand at kite surfing or join a snorkeling excursion right from your doorstep.

8. **Zanzibar Beach Resort**: Don't let the name fool you—Zanzibar Beach Resort offers hostel-style accommodations with resort-worthy amenities. Located on the serene shores of Jambiani Beach, this eco-conscious hostel features cozy beachfront bungalows, a communal kitchen, and a tranquil garden oasis perfect for lazy afternoons in the hammock.

9. **Che Che Vule Hostel**: Embrace the bohemian spirit of Nungwi at Che Che Vule Hostel, where vibrant colors and quirky decor set the stage for unforgettable adventures. With beachside bonfires, live music performances, and a bustling bar scene, this hostel is a hub of creativity and camaraderie. Get ready to make memories that last a lifetime!

10. **Paje Hostel & Kite Village**: Calling all water babies and kite surfing enthusiasts—Paje Hostel & Kite Village is your ultimate playground. Located steps away from Paje Beach, this hostel offers affordable accommodations, kite surfing lessons for all skill levels, and a lively beach bar scene where the party never stops. It's time to ride the wind and chase your kite surfing dreams!

Direction

1. **Chillax Hostel Zanzibar** Address: Malindi Road, Stone Town, Zanzibar Directions: From Zanzibar International Airport, take a taxi or a shared shuttle to Stone Town. Chillax Hostel is located on Malindi Road, just a short walk from the historic center.!

2. **Zanziplanet Hostel** Address: Nungwi Beach, Nungwi, Zanzibar Directions: From Stone Town, you can take a local dala-dala (minibus) or hire a taxi to Nungwi Beach. Zanziplanet Hostel is situated directly on the beachfront, near Nungwi Village.

3. **Lost & Found Hostel** Address: Jambiani Beach, Jambiani, Zanzibar Directions: To reach Jambiani, you can take a taxi or arrange a transfer from Stone Town. Lost & Found Hostel is located on Jambiani Beach, approximately 1 hour and 30 minutes from Stone Town.

4. **Savanna & Ocean** Address: Paje Beach, Paje, Zanzibar Directions: Paje is about a 1-hour drive from Stone Town. You can take a taxi or a dala-dala to Paje Beach. Savanna & Ocean Hostel is situated near Paje Beach, just a short walk from the main road

5. **Zanzibar Rock House** Address: 154 Malindi Road, Stone Town, Zanzibar Directions: Zanzibar Rock House is located in the heart of Stone Town, on Malindi Road. From Zanzibar International Airport, take a taxi or shuttle to Stone Town.

6. **Jambiani Guesthouse** Address: Jambiani Village, Jambiani, Zanzibar Directions: Jambiani Guesthouse is located in the village of Jambiani, approximately 1 hour and 30 minutes from Stone Town. You can take a taxi or arrange a transfer from Stone Town to Jambiani. The guesthouse is situated near the main road in the village.

7. **Paje by Night** Address: Paje Beach, Paje, Zanzibar Directions: Paje by Night Hostel is located directly on Paje Beach. From Stone Town, you can take a taxi or a dala-dala to Paje Beach. The hostel is situated near the beach access point, just a short walk from the main road.

8. **Zanzibar Beach Resort** Address: Jambiani Beach, Jambiani, Zanzibar Directions:

Zanzibar Beach Resort is located on Jambiani Beach, approximately 1 hour and 30 minutes from Stone Town. You can take a taxi or arrange a transfer from Stone Town to Jambiani. The resort is situated directly on the beachfront.

9. **Che Che Vule Hostel** Address: Nungwi Beach, Nungwi, Zanzibar Directions: Che Che Vule Hostel is located on Nungwi Beach, near the village of Nungwi. From Stone Town, you can take a taxi or a dala-dala to Nungwi Beach

10. **Paje Hostel & Kite Village** Address: Paje Beach, Paje, Zanzibar Directions: Paje Hostel & Kite Village is located directly on Paje Beach. From Stone Town, you can take a taxi or a dala-dala to Paje Beach

Direction

1. **Chillax Hostel Zanzibar** Address: Kenyatta Road, Stone Town, Zanzibar Directions: From Zanzibar International Airport, take a taxi or dala dala (local minibus) to Stone Town. Once in Stone Town, head towards Kenyatta Road. Chillax Hostel is located near the junction of Kenyatta Road and Gizenga Street, easily identifiable by its colorful exterior and rooftop terrace.

2. **Zanziplanet Hostel** Address: Nungwi Beach, Zanzibar Directions: From Zanzibar

International Airport, hire a taxi or arrange for a shuttle service to Nungwi Beach. Zanziplanet Hostel is situated directly on the beachfront, just a short walk from Nungwi Village. Look for the signboard along the beach indicating the hostel's entrance.

3. **Lost & Found Hostel** Address: Jambiani Beach, Zanzibar Directions: From Zanzibar International Airport, hire a taxi or arrange for transportation to Jambiani Beach on the southeast coast of the island. Lost & Found Hostel is located along the main road running parallel to the beach, easily accessible by foot or vehicle.

4. **Savanna & Ocean** Address: Paje, Zanzibar Directions: From Zanzibar International Airport, take a taxi or dala dala to Paje village on the southeast coast of the island. Savanna & Ocean Hostel is situated along the main road in Paje, just a short walk from the beach. Look for the colorful signage and lush garden entrance.

5. **Zanzibar Rock House** Address: Kenyatta Road, Stone Town, Zanzibar Directions: Zanzibar Rock House is conveniently located in the heart of Stone Town. From Zanzibar International Airport, take a taxi or dala dala to Stone Town. The hostel is situated on Kenyatta Road, near the junction of Kenyatta

Road and Gizenga Street, easily recognizable by its rooftop terrace and panoramic views.

6. **Jambiani Guesthouse** Address: Jambiani Village, Zanzibar Directions: From Zanzibar International Airport, hire a taxi or arrange for transportation to Jambiani village on the southeast coast of the island. Jambiani Guesthouse is located within the village, along the main road leading to the beach. Look for the signboard and entrance gate.

7. **Paje by Night** Address: Paje Beach, Zanzibar Directions: Paje by Night Hostel is situated directly on Paje Beach, on the southeast coast of Zanzibar. From Zanzibar International Airport, hire a taxi or arrange for transportation to Paje village. The hostel is located near the beachfront, easily identifiable by its beach bar and lounge area.

8. **Zanzibar Beach Resort** Address: Jambiani Beach, Zanzibar Directions: Zanzibar Beach Resort is located on Jambiani Beach, on the southeast coast of the island. From Zanzibar International Airport, take a taxi or arrange for transportation to Jambiani village. The resort is situated directly on the beachfront, with clear signage and beach access.

9. **Che Che Vule Hostel** Address: Nungwi Beach, Zanzibar Directions: From Zanzibar International Airport, hire a taxi or arrange

for transportation to Nungwi Beach on the northern tip of the island. Che Che Vule Hostel is located along the beachfront, just a short walk from Nungwi Village. Look for the colorful signage and beach bar area.

10. **Paje Hostel & Kite Village** Address: Paje Beach, Zanzibar Directions: Paje Hostel & Kite Village is situated directly on Paje Beach, on the southeast coast of Zanzibar. From Zanzibar International Airport, hire a taxi or arrange for transportation to Paje village. The hostel is located near the beachfront, with clear signage and kite surfing facilities

FINEST RESTAURANT AND CUISINE EXPERIENCES IN ZANZIBAR

TOP SAVORY DISHES IN ZANZIBAR

Ahoy, fellow foodie! Get ready to tantalize your taste buds with the top cuisine to try out in Zanzibar. From spicy seafood delicacies to sweet and savory treats, Zanzibari cuisine is a vibrant fusion of flavors influenced by Arabic, Indian, and African culinary traditions. So loosen your belt, prepare for a feast, and let's embark on a mouthwatering culinary adventure!

1. **Zanzibar Pizza**: Imagine a crispy, golden crust stuffed with a mouthwatering medley of ingredients like minced meat, vegetables, eggs, and cheese, all folded and fried to perfection. Zanzibar pizza is a must-try street food delight, best enjoyed hot and fresh from the grill at Forodhani Gardens in Stone Town. Don't forget to drizzle it with spicy sauce for an extra kick!

2. **Urojo**: Dive into a bowl of urojo, a tangy and spicy soup bursting with flavor and color. Made with a base of tangy tamarind broth and packed with ingredients like lentils, potatoes, onions, and fried snacks, urojo is a popular

street food dish that's perfect for cooling down on a hot day. Top it off with crunchy bhajias and crispy papri for an extra dose of texture and taste.

3. **Pilau**: Savor the aromatic flavors of pilau, a fragrant rice dish infused with spices like cinnamon, cardamom, cloves, and cumin. Cooked with meat or seafood and flavored with caramelized onions, garlic, and ginger, pilau is a staple of Swahili cuisine and a must-try dish for anyone visiting Zanzibar. Pair it with a side of kachumbari, a fresh tomato and onion salad, for a burst of freshness.

4. **Octopus Curry**: Indulge in the rich and flavorful taste of octopus curry, a beloved seafood dish that's a favorite among locals and visitors alike. Tender octopus simmered in a fragrant curry sauce made with coconut milk, tomatoes, and spices like turmeric, coriander, and chili, octopus curry is a true taste of Zanzibar's coastal flavors. Enjoy it with a side of rice or chapati for a hearty and satisfying meal.

5. **Zanzibari Mix**: Treat your taste buds to a culinary adventure with Zanzibar's famous Zanzibari mix, a tantalizing assortment of street food snacks and delicacies. From crispy samosas and crunchy bhajias to spicy kebabs and grilled seafood skewers, Zanzibari mix

offers a little something for everyone. Head to Forodhani Gardens in the evening to sample this mouthwatering array of flavors and textures.

6. **Mishkaki**: Sink your teeth into succulent skewers of mishkaki, tender chunks of marinated meat grilled to perfection over an open flame. Whether it's beef, chicken, or seafood, mishkaki is a popular street food dish in Zanzibar, beloved for its smoky flavor and spicy marinade. Enjoy it hot off the grill with a squeeze of fresh lime and a side of tangy tamarind sauce.

7. **Mchuzi wa Samaki**: Delight in the flavors of mchuzi wa samaki, a fragrant fish curry that's a staple of Zanzibari cuisine. Made with fresh catch of the day simmered in a rich and aromatic sauce made with coconut milk, tomatoes, onions, and spices like ginger, garlic, and chili, mchuzi wa samaki is a comforting and flavorful dish that pairs perfectly with rice or chapati.

8. **Biryani**: Transport your taste buds to India with a plate of biryani, a flavorful rice dish infused with aromatic spices and packed with tender meat or vegetables. Whether it's chicken, beef, or goat biryani, this beloved dish is a favorite among Zanzibar's residents and visitors alike. Served with a side of raita, a

cooling yogurt sauce, biryani is a satisfying and hearty meal that's perfect for sharing with friends and family.

9. **Mandazi**: Treat yourself to a sweet and fluffy mandazi, a popular snack that's enjoyed throughout East Africa. Resembling a doughnut or fried bread, mandazi is made with flour, sugar, coconut milk, and spices like cardamom and nutmeg, then fried until golden brown. Enjoy it with a cup of spicy chai for a delicious and comforting treat any time of day.

10. **Boku Boku**: Cool off with a refreshing glass of boku boku, a traditional Zanzibari drink made from fresh coconut water mixed with sugar and lime juice. Served chilled over ice, boku boku is the perfect way to beat the heat and quench your thirst after a day of exploring the island. Whether you're lounging on the beach or strolling through the streets of Stone Town, boku boku is a refreshing and revitalizing beverage that's sure to hit the spot.

10 BEST RESTAURANT IN ZANZIBAR

Ahoy, hungry traveler! Prepare to embark on a culinary adventure through the top restaurants in Zanzibar, where flavorful dishes and stunning settings await. From beachfront bistros to elegant eateries, these dining spots serve up a feast for the senses that will leave you craving more. So loosen your belt, sharpen your appetite, and let's dive into the delicious world of Zanzibari cuisine!

1. **The Rock Restaurant** Location: Michanvi Pingwe Beach, Zanzibar Menu: Start your meal with their signature seafood platter featuring fresh lobster, grilled prawns, and succulent fish, followed by their famous Zanzibar curry served with fluffy coconut rice. Don't miss the chance to indulge in their decadent chocolate lava cake for dessert—it's a true taste of paradise!

2. **Emerson Spice** Location: Tharia Street, Stone Town, Zanzibar Menu: Transport your taste buds to another era with Emerson Spice's fusion of Swahili and Arabic flavors. Begin your culinary journey with their tangy urojo soup, followed by their aromatic biryani rice served with tender lamb or chicken. For dessert, indulge in their homemade date and almond cake drizzled with honey—pure indulgence!

3. **The Tea House Restaurant** Location: 1911 Building, Shangani Street, Stone Town, Zanzibar Menu: Embark on a culinary adventure with The Tea House Restaurant's eclectic menu featuring Zanzibari classics and international favorites. Start with their refreshing Zanzibar salad featuring tropical

fruits and greens, followed by their mouthwatering seafood paella. Finish on a sweet note with their creamy mango cheesecake—a delightful treat for the senses!

4. **Jafferji's Royal Kitchen** Location: 170 Gizenga Street, Stone Town, Zanzibar Menu: Dive into the rich flavors of Zanzibar with Jafferji's Royal Kitchen's tantalizing menu. Begin your meal with their savory samosas stuffed with spiced potatoes and peas, followed by their aromatic fish tagine served with couscous. Save room for dessert and indulge in their decadent coconut and cardamom ice cream—it's the perfect ending to a memorable meal!

5. **Cinnamon Restaurant & Bar** Location: DoubleTree by Hilton Resort, Nungwi Beach, Zanzibar Menu: Treat yourself to a culinary feast at Cinnamon Restaurant & Bar, where the freshest seafood and local ingredients take center stage. Start with their seafood ceviche featuring marinated fish and tropical fruits, followed by their sumptuous lobster thermidor. For dessert, indulge in their passion fruit and coconut panna cotta—a symphony of flavors that will leave you craving more!

6. **Livingstone Beach Restaurant** Location: Kendwa Beach, Zanzibar Menu: Savor the

flavors of the ocean at Livingstone Beach Restaurant, where the catch of the day takes center stage. Begin your meal with their crispy calamari served with tangy lemon aioli, followed by their mouthwatering seafood linguine tossed in a garlic and herb sauce. For dessert, indulge in their refreshing coconut sorbet—it's the perfect way to end a beachfront feast!

7. **Upendo Zanzibar** Location: Matemwe Beach, Zanzibar Menu: Experience the true essence of Zanzibari cuisine at Upendo Zanzibar, where traditional flavors meet modern twists. Start with their flavorful octopus curry served with coconut rice, followed by their fragrant pilau rice served with juicy grilled prawns. For dessert, treat yourself to their indulgent chocolate fondant—a decadent finale to an unforgettable meal!

8. **The Beach House** Location: Bwejuu Beach, Zanzibar Menu: Escape to culinary paradise at The Beach House, where the tranquil setting complements the mouthwatering menu. Begin your meal with their refreshing watermelon and feta salad, followed by their flavorful seafood tagliatelle. For dessert, indulge in their creamy tiramisu—a heavenly treat that will leave you craving more!

9. **Sea Cliff Restaurant** Location: Sea Cliff Resort & Spa, Mbweni, Zanzibar Menu: Indulge in a culinary journey at Sea Cliff Restaurant, where international flavors are infused with local ingredients. Start with their savory beef carpaccio served with rocket salad, followed by their succulent grilled lobster served with garlic butter. For dessert, treat yourself to their classic crème brûlée—a perfect ending to a memorable meal!

10. **Forodhani Gardens** Location: Forodhani Gardens, Stone Town, Zanzibar Menu: Explore the vibrant flavors of Zanzibar at Forodhani Gardens, where local vendors serve up a tantalizing array of street food delights. Sample freshly grilled seafood skewers, savory Zanzibar pizzas, and sweet treats like sugarcane juice and coconut ice cream. With its lively atmosphere and diverse offerings, Forodhani Gardens is a must-visit culinary destination in Zanzibar!

Direction

1. **The Rock Restaurant** Address: Michanvi Pingwe Beach, Zanzibar Directions: The Rock Restaurant is located on Michanvi Pingwe Beach, a picturesque spot on the southeastern coast of Zanzibar. From Stone Town, it's approximately a 1.5-hour drive by taxi or private car. Once you arrive at the beach,

you'll see The Rock perched on a large rock formation just off the shore. During low tide, you can walk to the restaurant, but during high tide, a small boat will ferry you across.

2. **Emerson Spice** Address: Tharia Street, Stone Town, Zanzibar Directions: Emerson Spice is located in the heart of Stone Town, Zanzibar's historic district. From Zanzibar International Airport, it's approximately a 15-minute drive by taxi or dala dala (local minibus) to Tharia Street. The restaurant is housed within the Emerson Spice Hotel, a beautifully restored mansion with ornate Arabesque architecture.

3. **The Tea House Restaurant** Address: 1911 Building, Shangani Street, Stone Town, Zanzibar Directions: The Tea House Restaurant is located within the 1911 Building on Shangani Street, a bustling thoroughfare in Stone Town. From Zanzibar International Airport, it's approximately a 15-minute drive by taxi or dala dala to Shangani Street. Look for the 1911 Building's distinctive colonial-style facade.

4. **Jafferji's Royal Kitchen** Address: 170 Gizenga Street, Stone Town, Zanzibar Directions: Jafferji's Royal Kitchen is located on Gizenga Street, one of the main streets in Stone Town. From Zanzibar International

Airport, it's approximately a 15-minute drive by taxi or dala dala to Gizenga Street. The restaurant is housed within the Jafferji House & Spa, a boutique hotel with a distinctive Zanzibari design.

5. **Cinnamon Restaurant & Bar** Address: DoubleTree by Hilton Resort, Nungwi Beach, Zanzibar Directions: Cinnamon Restaurant & Bar is located within the DoubleTree by Hilton Resort on Nungwi Beach, a popular tourist destination on the northern coast of Zanzibar. From Zanzibar International Airport, it's approximately a 1-hour drive by taxi or private car to Nungwi Beach. The restaurant is situated within the resort complex, overlooking the beach.

6. **Livingstone Beach Restaurant** Address: Kendwa Beach, Zanzibar Directions: Livingstone Beach Restaurant is located on Kendwa Beach, one of the most beautiful beaches on the northern coast of Zanzibar. From Zanzibar International Airport, it's approximately a 1-hour drive by taxi or private car to Kendwa Beach. The restaurant is situated directly on the beach, with stunning views of the Indian Ocean.

7. **Upendo Zanzibar** Address: Matemwe Beach, Zanzibar Directions: Upendo Zanzibar is located on Matemwe Beach, a secluded

stretch of coastline on the northeastern coast of Zanzibar. From Zanzibar International Airport, it's approximately a 1.5-hour drive by taxi or private car to Matemwe Beach. The restaurant is situated within the Upendo Zanzibar Lodge, a boutique hotel overlooking the ocean.

8. **The Beach House** Address: Bwejuu Beach, Zanzibar Directions: The Beach House is located on Bwejuu Beach, a pristine stretch of sand on the southeastern coast of Zanzibar. From Zanzibar International Airport, it's approximately a 1-hour drive by taxi or private car to Bwejuu Beach. The restaurant is situated directly on the beach, with stunning views of the Indian Ocean

9. **Sea Cliff Restaurant** Address: Sea Cliff Resort & Spa, Mbweni, Zanzibar Directions: Sea Cliff Restaurant is located within the Sea Cliff Resort & Spa, a luxurious hotel overlooking the ocean in Mbweni, just outside Stone Town. From Zanzibar International Airport, it's approximately a 20-minute drive by taxi or private car to Mbweni. The restaurant is situated within the resort complex, with panoramic views of the coastline.

10. **Forodhani Gardens** Address: Forodhani Gardens, Stone Town, Zanzibar

Directions: Forodhani Gardens is located in the heart of Stone Town, adjacent to the Old Fort and the House of Wonders. From Zanzibar International Airport, it's approximately a 15-minute drive by taxi or dala dala to Stone Town. The gardens are situated along the waterfront, with food stalls set up in the evenings.

VIBRANT NIGHTLIFE AND FESTIVITY IN ZANZIBAR

Ahoy, night owls! Prepare to dance the night away and soak up the vibrant nightlife of Zanzibar. From beachside bars to pulsating clubs, this island paradise comes alive after dark with beats, drinks, and good vibes. So slip into your dancing shoes, grab your favorite cocktail, and let's explore the top clubs and nightlife hotspots that Zanzibar has to offer!

1. **Livingstone Beach Bar & Nightclub** Location: Kendwa Beach, Zanzibar Description: Kick off your night at Livingstone Beach Bar & Nightclub, where the beats are hot, and the drinks are cold. Located on the pristine shores of Kendwa Beach, this open-air club offers panoramic views of the Indian Ocean and a lively atmosphere that's perfect for dancing under the stars. With resident DJs spinning the latest tracks and themed parties that keep the energy levels soaring, Livingstone is the ultimate party destination in Zanzibar.

2. **Red Monkey Lodge** Location: Jambiani Beach, Zanzibar Description: Escape to the laid-back vibes of Red Monkey Lodge, a beachfront oasis that's home to one of Zanzibar's coolest nightlife spots. Nestled on the shores of Jambiani Beach, this eclectic

lodge boasts a vibrant bar and lounge area where travelers from around the world come together to share stories, sip cocktails, and dance to the rhythms of live music and DJ sets. Whether you're chilling in a hammock or grooving on the dance floor, Red Monkey Lodge is the place to be for a relaxed yet unforgettable night out.

3. **Safari Blue Club** Location: Nungwi Beach, Zanzibar Description: Experience the magic of Zanzibar's nightlife at Safari Blue Club, a beachside venue where the party never stops. Located on the lively shores of Nungwi Beach, this club offers a perfect blend of tropical vibes, delicious cocktails, and pulsating beats that will keep you dancing until the early hours of the morning. With fire shows, themed parties, and guest DJs adding to the excitement, Safari Blue Club is a must-visit destination for party animals and beach lovers alike.

4. **Zanzibar Rock** Location: Kenyatta Road, Stone Town, Zanzibar Description: Get ready to rock the night away at Zanzibar Rock, a legendary nightclub in the heart of Stone Town. Housed in a historic building on Kenyatta Road, this iconic venue boasts multiple dance floors, VIP lounges, and state-of-the-art sound and lighting systems that create an unforgettable party atmosphere.

Whether you're into house, hip-hop, or afrobeat, Zanzibar Rock has something for everyone, with resident DJs and guest artists keeping the dance floor packed until the early hours.

5. **Waikiki Beach Club** Location: Paje Beach, Zanzibar Description: Escape to paradise at Waikiki Beach Club, a beachfront venue that's all about sun, sand, and good vibes. Located on the golden shores of Paje Beach, this laid-back club offers a relaxed atmosphere where you can kick back with a cocktail in hand and soak up the tropical ambiance. With live music, bonfire parties, and beachside BBQs adding to the excitement, Waikiki Beach Club is the perfect spot to unwind and let loose after a day of exploring Zanzibar.

6. **Sunset Lounge** Location: Nungwi Beach, Zanzibar Description: Catch the sunset and party into the night at Sunset Lounge, a chic beachfront venue with a laid-back vibe and stunning views. Perched on the shores of Nungwi Beach, this stylish lounge offers a relaxed setting where you can sip cocktails, sample delicious tapas, and dance to the sounds of resident DJs spinning chilled-out beats and feel-good tunes. Whether you're lounging on a bean bag or hitting the dance floor, Sunset Lounge is the ultimate spot to

unwind and enjoy the beauty of Zanzibar's nightlife.

7. **Moonshine Beach Bar** Location: Paje Beach, Zanzibar Description: Experience the magic of a moonlit beach party at Moonshine Beach Bar, a lively venue nestled on the shores of Paje Beach. With its laid-back atmosphere, colorful decor, and eclectic music selection, this beach bar offers a relaxed setting where you can kick back with a cocktail and dance the night away under the stars. Whether you're chilling in a hammock or showing off your dance moves on the sand, Moonshine Beach Bar is the place to be for a memorable night out in Zanzibar.

8. **Babylon Nightclub** Location: Malindi, Stone Town, Zanzibar Description: Step into the vibrant world of Babylon Nightclub, a popular spot for locals and tourists alike to dance, drink, and socialize until the early hours. Located in the lively neighborhood of Malindi in Stone Town, this energetic club features multiple dance floors, live bands, and resident DJs playing a mix of Afrobeat, reggae, and hip-hop tunes. With its colorful decor, friendly atmosphere, and late-night parties, Babylon Nightclub guarantees a night to remember in Zanzibar.

9. **Coco Beach Club** Location: Jambiani Beach, Zanzibar Description: Immerse yourself in the laid-back vibes of Coco Beach Club, a beachfront venue that's all about good times and great music. Located on the shores of Jambiani Beach, this chilled-out club offers a relaxed setting where you can sip cocktails, mingle with fellow travelers, and dance to the sounds of live bands and DJs. With its cozy seating areas, beachfront bonfires, and stunning ocean views, Coco Beach Club is the perfect spot to unwind and enjoy the beauty of Zanzibar's nightlife.

10. **Zanzibar Queen Hotel Rooftop Bar** Location: Gizenga Street, Stone Town, Zanzibar Description: Elevate your night out at the Zanzibar Queen Hotel Rooftop Bar, where stunning views and stylish ambiance come together to create an unforgettable experience. Located in the heart of Stone Town, this rooftop bar offers panoramic views of the city skyline and the Indian Ocean, making it the perfect spot to watch the sunset and enjoy a nightcap. With its cozy seating areas, creative cocktails, and laid-back vibe, the Zanzibar Queen Hotel Rooftop Bar is the ultimate destination for a memorable night out in Zanzibar.

Direction

1. **Livingstone Beach Bar & Nightclub** Address: Kendwa Beach, Zanzibar

2. **Red Monkey Lodge** Address: Jambiani Beach, Zanzibar.

3. **Safari Blue Club** Address: Nungwi Beach, Zanzibar

4. **Zanzibar Rock** Address: Kenyatta Road, Stone Town, Zanzibar

5. **Waikiki Beach Club** Address: Paje Beach, Zanzibar

6. **Sunset Lounge** Address: Nungwi Beach, Zanzibar

7. **Moonshine Beach Bar** Address: Paje Beach, Zanzibar

8. **Babylon Nightclub** Address: Malindi, Stone Town, Zanzibar

9. **Coco Beach Club** Address: Jambiani Beach, Zanzibar

10. **Zanzibar Queen Hotel Rooftop Bar** Address: Gizenga Street, Stone Town, Zanzibar

FESTIVE CELEBRATIONS IN ZANZIBAR

Ahoy, festival-goers! Get ready to immerse yourself in the vibrant culture and lively celebrations of Zanzibar. From colorful parades to traditional music and dance, this island paradise knows how to throw a party like no other. So dust off your dancing shoes, don your festive attire, and let's dive into the exciting world of Zanzibar's festivals and celebrations!

1. **Zanzibar International Film Festival (ZIFF)**: Lights, camera, action! The Zanzibar International Film Festival (ZIFF) is a star-studded event that celebrates the best of African cinema and showcases the talents of filmmakers from around the world. Held annually in Stone Town, this week-long festival features film screenings, workshops, panel discussions, and cultural events that highlight the rich diversity of African storytelling. From thought-provoking documentaries to heartwarming dramas, ZIFF offers something for every cinephile to enjoy.

2. **Sauti za Busara Festival**: Get ready to dance to the rhythm of Africa at the Sauti za Busara Festival, one of East Africa's largest and most vibrant music festivals. Held annually in Stone Town, this four-day

89

extravaganza celebrates the best of African music and culture, with live performances by artists from across the continent. From traditional taarab music to contemporary afro-pop, reggae, and hip-hop, Sauti za Busara offers a diverse lineup of musical genres that will have you dancing in the streets until dawn.

3. **Mwaka Kogwa Festival**: Experience the fiery spirit of the Mwaka Kogwa Festival, a traditional celebration of the Shirazi New Year held in the village of Makunduchi. This colorful festival features ritualistic activities such as mock battles, drumming, and dancing, as well as traditional games and feasting. The highlight of the festival is the symbolic burning of thatched huts, which is believed to ward off evil spirits and bring good luck for the year ahead. Join in the festivities and witness the unique cultural traditions of Zanzibar come to life in Makunduchi.

4. **Eid al-Fitr and Eid al-Adha**: Join the local Muslim community in celebrating Eid al-Fitr and Eid al-Adha, two of the most important religious festivals in Islam. Eid al-Fitr marks the end of Ramadan, the holy month of fasting, with prayers, feasting, and charitable giving. Eid al-Adha, also known as the Festival of Sacrifice, commemorates the

willingness of Ibrahim (Abraham) to sacrifice his son as an act of obedience to God, with prayers, animal sacrifices, and communal meals. Experience the spirit of unity, generosity, and compassion as the people of Zanzibar come together to celebrate these joyous occasions.

5. **Zanzibar Food Festival**: Prepare your taste buds for a culinary adventure at the Zanzibar Food Festival, a mouthwatering celebration of the island's rich culinary heritage. Held annually in Stone Town, this week-long event features cooking demonstrations, food tastings, and culinary competitions showcasing the best of Zanzibari cuisine. From spicy seafood delicacies to sweet and savory treats, the Zanzibar Food Festival offers a feast for the senses that will leave you craving more.

6. **Karume Day**: Pay tribute to the legacy of Zanzibar's first president, Abeid Amani Karume, on Karume Day, a public holiday celebrated annually on April 7th. This day honors Karume's contributions to the struggle for independence and his efforts to promote unity, equality, and social justice in Zanzibar. Join in the festivities with parades, speeches, and cultural performances that celebrate Karume's life and legacy, and

reflect on the values of peace, freedom, and democracy that he championed.

7. **Zanzibar International Music Festival (ZIMF)**: Get ready to groove to the beat at the Zanzibar International Music Festival (ZIMF), a lively celebration of music, dance, and culture held annually in Stone Town. This multi-day event features live performances by local and international artists representing a wide range of musical genres, from traditional taarab and ngoma to contemporary jazz, funk, and fusion. With its electrifying atmosphere and diverse lineup of talent, ZIMF offers a one-of-a-kind experience that will have you dancing in the streets all night long.

8. **Zanzibar Revolution Day**: Commemorate the anniversary of Zanzibar's Revolution on January 12th, a public holiday that marks the overthrow of the Sultanate of Zanzibar in 1964. This day honors the brave men and women who fought for independence and social justice, and celebrates the founding principles of the Zanzibar Revolution, including equality, democracy, and self-determination. Join in the commemorations with parades, speeches, and cultural performances that reflect on the history and significance of this pivotal moment in Zanzibar's past.

9. **Ngoma Festival**: Experience the rhythm of Zanzibar's traditional music and dance at the Ngoma Festival, a vibrant celebration of Swahili culture held annually in various locations across the island. This multi-day event features performances by local dance troupes, drummers, and musicians showcasing traditional ngoma (dance) styles such as mdundiko, beni, and kidumbak. Join in the festivities with dance workshops, drum circles, and cultural exhibitions that highlight the rich diversity of Zanzibari heritage.

EXPLORING ZANZIBAR SHOPPING AND SOUVENIR

TOP SHOPPING PLACES IN ZANZIBAR

Ahoy, fellow treasure hunters! Prepare to embark on a shopping adventure through the vibrant markets and boutique shops of Zanzibar, where exotic treasures and unique souvenirs await. From intricate handicrafts to fragrant spices and colorful fabrics, this island paradise offers a treasure trove of shopping delights that will leave you spoilt for choice. So grab your shopping bag, sharpen your bargaining skills, and let's dive into the bustling world of Zanzibar's shopping destinations and souvenirs!

1. **Darajani Market**: Step into the heart of Stone Town and discover the bustling bazaar known as Darajani Market, where locals and visitors alike come to shop for fresh produce, spices, and handmade goods. Navigate through narrow alleyways filled with stalls selling everything from ripe mangoes and exotic fruits to aromatic spices like cloves, cinnamon, and vanilla. Don't miss the chance to sample local delicacies like Zanzibar pizza and sugar cane juice as you explore this vibrant market maze.

2. **Forodhani Night Market**: As the sun sets over Stone Town, head to Forodhani Gardens and experience the culinary delights of Forodhani Night Market, a lively food market where vendors grill, fry, and skewer a mouthwatering array of seafood, meats, and snacks. Sample street food favorites like grilled lobster, seafood kebabs, and Zanzibar pizzas stuffed with spicy fillings, then wash it all down with a refreshing sugarcane juice or freshly squeezed juice from a coconut. With its bustling atmosphere and delicious offerings, Forodhani Night Market is a must-visit destination for foodies and adventurers alike.

3. **Mangapwani Slave Caves Souvenir Market**: Dive into history and culture at the Mangapwani Slave Caves Souvenir Market, located near the site of a historic slave cave complex on the north coast of Zanzibar. Browse through a variety of locally made handicrafts, including intricately carved wooden sculptures, colorful textiles, and beaded jewelry, all crafted by skilled artisans using traditional techniques. Pick up unique souvenirs like miniature dhows, coconut shell ornaments, and handmade soapstone carvings to commemorate your visit to this historic site.

4. **Mrembo Spa Boutique**: Treat yourself to a pampering session at Mrembo Spa Boutique, a tranquil oasis located in the heart of Stone

Town. Browse through a curated selection of natural skincare products, including organic soaps, lotions, and oils made with locally sourced ingredients like coconut, shea butter, and seaweed. Indulge in a luxurious spa treatment using traditional Zanzibari techniques, such as a seaweed body wrap or a Swahili spice massage, and take home a piece of island paradise to enjoy long after your vacation is over.

5. **Zanzibar Curio Shop**: Step into the colorful world of Zanzibar Curio Shop and discover a treasure trove of souvenirs and gifts that capture the spirit of the island. Browse through shelves filled with handcrafted goods, including beaded sandals, woven baskets, and carved wooden figurines depicting local wildlife and cultural motifs. Admire the intricate designs of traditional kangas and kikoys, colorful textiles worn by locals for special occasions, and pick out a few to add a touch of Zanzibari flair to your wardrobe.

6. **Spice Farms and Plantations**: Embark on a sensory journey through the spice farms and plantations of Zanzibar, where fragrant spices like cloves, nutmeg, and cinnamon are cultivated in abundance. Take a guided tour of a spice farm and learn about the cultivation and harvesting process of these exotic ingredients, then visit the farm's gift shop to

purchase freshly ground spices, aromatic oils, and handmade spice blends to take home with you. Don't forget to pick up a few packets of Zanzibar's famous vanilla pods or saffron threads to add a touch of island flavor to your cooking back home.

7. **Zenji House Boutique**: Discover the hidden gems of Zanzibar's artisanal scene at Zenji House Boutique, a charming shop located in the heart of Stone Town. Browse through racks of handcrafted clothing and accessories made from locally sourced fabrics, including brightly colored kangas, kikoys, and batik prints. Admire the intricate beadwork and embroidery of traditional Maasai jewelry, and pick out a few pieces to add a pop of color and culture to your wardrobe. Don't forget to check out the shop's selection of handmade home decor items, including woven baskets, carved wooden masks, and hand-painted ceramics, to bring a piece of Zanzibar's vibrant culture into your home.

8. **Nakupenda Beach Market**: Escape the hustle and bustle of Stone Town and head to Nakupenda Beach Market, a hidden gem located on the shores of Prison Island. Browse through stalls selling a variety of handmade goods, including beaded jewelry, tie-dye clothing, and woven baskets, all crafted by local artisans using traditional techniques.

Relax on the beach with a refreshing coconut water in hand as you shop for souvenirs and soak up the laid-back island vibes of Nakupenda Beach Market.

9. **Kisiwa on the Beach Boutique**: Treat yourself to a shopping spree at Kisiwa on the Beach Boutique, a stylish shop located in the heart of Paje Beach. Browse through racks of bohemian-inspired clothing and accessories, including flowy dresses, embroidered tunics, and beaded sandals, perfect for a day of beachside lounging or exploring the island. Admire the intricate beadwork and craftsmanship of Maasai jewelry, and pick out a few statement pieces to add a touch of island chic to your wardrobe.

10. **Jozani Chwaka Bay National Park Visitor Center**: Immerse yourself in nature and culture at the Jozani Chwaka Bay National Park Visitor Center, where you'll find a selection of souvenirs and gifts inspired by Zanzibar's rich biodiversity. Browse through shelves filled with books, postcards, and educational materials about the park's flora and fauna, then pick out a few eco-friendly souvenirs, such as handmade paper products, recycled glassware, and organic cotton clothing, to support conservation efforts and take home a piece of Zanzibar's natural beauty.

CONCLUSION

As we draw the final curtain on our journey through the pages of the ZANZIBAR TRAVEL GUIDE 2024 UPDATED, let's take a moment to savor the memories we've created, the adventures we've embarked upon, and the countless wonders of Zanzibar we've uncovered together.

From the sun-kissed shores of pristine beaches to the labyrinthine alleyways of historic Stone Town, our exploration of Zanzibar has been nothing short of extraordinary. We've basked in the warmth of the Indian Ocean, marveled at the grandeur of ancient architecture, and danced to the rhythm of Swahili culture under the stars.

But beyond the breathtaking landscapes and tantalizing cuisine, it's the people of Zanzibar who have truly stolen our hearts. Their warmth, hospitality, and boundless generosity have enriched our journey in ways we never could have imagined. From the humble vendors at the market to the skilled artisans crafting souvenirs with love, each encounter has left an indelible mark on our souls.

As we bid farewell to this enchanting island paradise, let us carry with us the spirit of Zanzibar – a spirit of resilience, diversity, and unbridled joy. Let us cherish the memories we've made and the friendships we've forged, knowing that our adventures in Zanzibar will live on in our hearts forever.

To each and every traveler who has turned the pages of this guide and embarked on their own Zanzibar adventure, we extend our heartfelt gratitude. Thank you for allowing us to be a part of your journey, for embracing the beauty of Zanzibar, and for daring to dream of new horizons.

As you venture forth into the world, may you carry the spirit of Zanzibar with you – a beacon of hope, inspiration, and boundless possibility. And may your travels be filled with wonder, discovery, and moments of pure magic.

From the bottom of our hearts, asante sana (thank you very much), and may your next adventure be even more magnificent than the last. Kwaheri ya kuonana (goodbye for now), dear traveler, until we meet again on the shores of Zanzibar.

[Alexander Scott]